ASKFIRMATIONS

Live the life you desire
simply by asking

CHRIS ALEXANDRIA

ISBN: 1499675305
ISBN-13: 9781499675306

iii

DEDICATION

I dedicate this book to YOU, a glorious being who is
just chomping at the bit to have a life filled with
joy, love, health, abundance (on all levels)
combined with the confidence and self-esteem
that you are worthy of it all!

Guideposts along the way:

    i.   backstory

   ii.   how it all came to be

  iii.   intro

  iv.   mind fodder

   v.   ego

  vi.   ASKFIRMATIONS defined

 vii.   the Askfirmation formula

viii.   creating ASKFIRMATIONS

  ix.   follow up

ACKNOWLEDGMENTS

I wish to lovingly and sincerely thank my Facebook group, Angel Chatter, for its non-stop support and constant willingness to step up and be my guinea pigs. Without you, my Dearest Chatterers, we'd still be wondering if ASKFIRMATIONS worked!

Thanks to Jim, wherever you now are, for inspiring me to write this book to begin with.

Thanks to Kim and Andrew Nock of Nock Photography for making my photo shoots so much fun and such a success.

Mostly, to my Honey Guy, you are my rock, my love and without whom I'd still be scampering around that gerbil wheel!

i. intro

My story is not one of a down-trodden life or of a rise from rags to riches. You can check up on this if you want. You'll see that I've been fortunate – I've always had decent clothes to wear, even if my mother attempted to copy the coolest fashions on her sewing machine to save a few precious dollars while keeping her teenage daughters looking respectable.

While I've been blessed to always live in comfort, with a sound roof over my head, plenty to eat and so forth, extreme excess has never knocked on my door. Likewise, I've never had one of those defining events, a near death experience, an epiphany, or any divine moment when everything became so crystal clear that I KNEW at that very moment what my destiny was to be. Instead, my path has been rather more of a slow dance, a *pas de deux* if you will, of grace and motion, with a sprinkling of tiny, yet empowering *Aha's* along the way.

My upbringing was rather idyllic, I'm happy to say, even decades later. I was lucky to be born to great parents, with great siblings, great grand-parents, aunts, uncles and assorted pseudo-relatives, all who loved, adored and supported me. I will go so far to say that all of them encouraged me, as well, no matter what my endeavor was at the moment. This collection of close and distant family was marked with incredibly innate intelligence and supremely high integrity.

Oh, and their creative barometer? Off the charts. Honestly - how many of you have watched the ants play baseball?

My paternal grandfather would take us children out into the yard and describe the play-by-play that we otherwise would have thought was just a bunch of ants jiggering around in the dirt. Maybe it was the loss of his beloved Dodgers to the west coast that made him such an avid fan of this very minor league, but he managed to draw us into the action for all nine innings . . . and we loved it! He kept at it, almost to the day he died, enthralling my children with balls, strikes and home runs right in the dirt behind his house in New Jersey. Oh, and then there were the submarine races and dinosaur hunts.

Yes, my beloved grandpa had a child's sense of wonder and imagination, and this same characteristic seemed to flow through my entire family. Now, some may think of this behavior as a little odd. Perhaps. I know I enjoyed this random streak in my relatives, but when it came to being "odd," I soon realized the one who was really a bit "off" was me. Really. Even in this bunch.

I was different.

Well what child doesn't think he or she is, right?

My difference, however, was a bit more on the unusual side. I could talk with angels. Not just listen to their one way messages, but converse or, as my daughter later explained it for me, "chat" with the angels. How many people do you know that chat with angels, freely admit it, and promote it?

Me included.

Seriously, it wasn't something that was part of a typical dinner table conversation in my house, growing up. Can you imagine me jumping in over the meatloaf or salmon cakes with the latest message from Auriel or Michael? Instead of asking how school was that day, what if my parents asked, "So, Chris, what angels did you chat with today?

How are they doing? Any insights you want to give us?"

Yeahhh . . . ummm . . .no. I don't think so. My wonderful parents were not THAT imaginative.

What was worse – in the beginning, I didn't even know that those voices I heard, telling me this, or guiding me here, were angels. I had no idea what they were and, at that early age, I hadn't been exposed to Joan of Arc, Bernadette of Lourdes, or other "angel chatterers" (my term, not theirs). I didn't know there were people around the world whose conversations with angels were "documented," and considered normal in their world. Okay, so one got burned at the stake for her 'normalcy', but she stayed true to her course and never wavered. Yeah, I was a bit different - I wavered and wavered BIG time.

After all, I was still a young girl and didn't understand what was going on, Instead, afraid that there was something seriously wrong with me, I clammed up. I shoved this little secret of mine so far down, drove it from my consciousness, that it didn't see the light of day for decades. This response was clearly a defense mechanism, created by the rationale of 'fitting in.' Like any other youngster, I craved to be normal and liked socially.

As a result of this suppression, I developed a nervous twitch when I was under stress. This behavior worsened to the point that my parents took me in for medical tests to make sure there was nothing medically wrong. Of course there wasn't, but that's how much my parents loved me - only wanting the best AND making sure I was A-OK (yeah, I know, to some, the jury is probably still out on that one). However, these tests proved to me that there was nothing really wrong with me, but the twitch persisted as I further drove my little ol' secret to the bottom of the well.

I went on this way, knowing things, *twitch,* hearing voices, *twitch*, and being unsure what to do or what it all meant, *twitch, twitch*. I tried to ignore the reaction and focused on what I was hearing. Given my natural gifts of intuition and healing, I was always sensitive to others around me; what they were feeling and how to offer that word of comfort, a hug, a loving ear, a smile. I always noticed how what they would say about themselves would eventually manifest, or not ~ all depending on what their self-talk was. It's the ol' universal law that words and thoughts have power.

But I was six or seven, so what did I know? How was I to understand that the Law of Attraction was alive and well even w-a-a-a-a-y back then before it was popular. Or that it was even called the Law of Attraction for that matter.

Ironically, no matter how much I suppressed the existence of my gifts and *tried* my best to fit in, it was futile. 'Friends' would support me with a wink, a nod and more than a bit of sarcasm. Sure, there were some that knew my 'dirty little secret', but not many. Life went on that way for years. This is not an 'Oh Woe Is Me' complaint, just the facts. I point this out because it shows we really can't be someone we aren't no matter how much we wish otherwise.

During those early years, into my twenties, perhaps, only a very few ever really supported me in the truest sense of the word and are still with me. You know who you are and I give thanks for your friendship daily. Eventually, I decided to come out of the closet and embrace my gifts as a blessing rather than a curse. At that juncture, many of my friends moved away from me, making way for the true ones to enter, take up residency and stay. 'Coming out of the closet' in itself was the ultimate game changer. Luckily for me, the voices have continued but, thankfully, the twitching has all but ceased since I began walking life on my terms. More on this in another book . . . (yes that was a tease), but it's an early acknowledgement that ASKFIRMATIONS, the subject of this book, have helped me feel safe in ways I never imagined.

As I matured, I met the love of my life. We married and raised some truly wonderful children. During those years of focus on family and hearth, those voices inside of my head had eased into the background, I think to allow me the freedom to tend to my duties as a wife and mother. Life continued to be idyllic, but deep down I was not entirely satisfied with life. I sensed there was something more I was to do besides making monkey bread, cleaning house and 'stuff.' Even so, in looking back, I would never – repeat never – have traded those times for anything.

I LOVED being a stay-at-home mom.

I LOVED being a domestic goddess.

I LOVED my life, but as our children aged, their dependency on me shifted and I was no longer the center of their universe.

It was time to find a way back to *me*.

In fact, one of my daughters, in her infinite wisdom, asked me at some point, "Mommy, you know we're not going to be living with you forever; what are you going to do then?"

Out of the mouths of babes.

That's when the angels came back full throttle into my life. I became insatiable for any and all information and stories that touched on the angelic realm. I subscribed to magazines, read books, read more books, went to psychics, even took classes. All leading to -- who knows?

In fact my honey would often – I repeat OFTEN – ask, "What are you going to do with *this* course?"

My response was typically, "I dunno... but have to take it."

He would then ask, "Are you planning on seeing clients?"

"Dunno."

"How is this going to help you?"

"Pfft . . ." was my ultimate answer.

No, my guy was a corporate finance professional,

where everything had a top and bottom line, and every investment was supposed to generate some form of payback. So, this was difficult for him to understand or rationalize. Nevertheless, he would smile at me, shake his head and, of course, clear his calendar to make sure I could get to the class with a clear conscious.

Talk about loving trust!

Yes, I was the sponge of the world and gladly took it all in, even though I didn't have a clue to where this was all leading.

Doors began to creak open. Many and tiny *AHA*s followed.

I began to see clients for energy and healing treatments. I had become a Reiki Master/Teacher during the 'Dunno Years'. I added IET Master/Teacher and a Magnified Healer to my skill sets. I studied crystals and became a licensed crystal therapist. I studied more and became an Archangel Enlightenment Therapist and Certified Soul Coach. I was able to use all of these modalities with my growing list of clients, and they LOVED me, and what I could do for them or teach them.

Yes! – at last I found I was good at something besides making monkey bread!

More importantly:

I LOVED helping people!

I LOVED offering them insights and tools that would keep them going long after our sessions were over.

I LOVED seeing their successes as their lives moved forward!

Little did I know where it would all eventually lead.

My gifts were literally magnifying, and so was my confidence and self-worth. Even so, I was still very hesitant to publicly state what I did to those outside of my personal circle of friends and colleagues who were familiar with energy healing and therapies. This stuff was still relatively unknown and scary for many; especially most that we associated with at cocktail parties or social gatherings.. I mostly kept up my guard and either played the dutiful corporate wife or interested social butterfly/mom when with my honey and his business colleagues, or amongst our neighbors at dinner outings or barbecues.

On those rare occasions during which I would speak about my angelic connection, I would get shocked looks of incredulity from the person with whom I was speaking. It was as if a set of horns had sprouted from my scalp, or an extra pair of eyes had bulged out of their sockets on my forehead. *"Clang, clang, clang! Calling the men in the white jackets please!"* In any case, these reactions did nothing to confirm that I was safe to share who I truly was.

After a few of these reactions by the uninformed and uninterested, I learned to steer my conversations away from such topics and nicely segue the talk to some work of art or piece of furniture (I found that the "oooh shiny" technique of distraction worked well). In this manner, I was able to escape stepping up to the platform and avoid getting the guaranteed 'weirdo' look, the silent "Airy Faery," or "Space Cadet" tag, or the hurried "Okaaayyyy, I'm sorry, but my husband/wife wants me" response as they ran away as fast as their feet would carry them.

Despite all of the positive feedback I was getting from my clients and others within my sphere, these "mainstream" incidents usually left me feeling less confident and not altogether happy.

Why weren't there more people out there that would get what I was saying?

There had to be other Chatterers out there, right?

Was I truly the odd man – okay in this case – odd Goddess out?

Ohhhh, woe is me! This time, I was really beginning to feel a bit sorry for myself.

Then I realized that I was doing a tremendous amount of not-so-nice "self-talk," that self-denigrating bit of inner conversation that we all fall into from time to time. So, I began to say mantras and affirmations; positive statements, about myself and life. I saw some results; but not enough that proved I was safe to be me. That I too could be extremely abundant and happy and joyful and healthy - you know how affirmations go.

In time, I met a few more people who got me, understood who I was and what I could do, and could even appreciate me. This was at least an improvement, though a *very* small one. But, I saw no golden path open before me that led the way to my personal Mecca. There were no neon signs on Broadway glowing, no blinking arrows pointing the way. If truth be told, there was barely a glimmer of confirmation that I was on the right track; nothing was really justifying me and informing me of my next steps, where to go, how to get there and with whom I should travel.

Little did I know that my answer was just down the road, both literally and figuratively. There was a move in our future that was about to inform me how to alter this chatter and get on with things. Despite what I said at the beginning, my epiphany was about to present itself and, true to form, its manifestation was like nothing I expected.

Chris Alexandria

ii. how it all came to be

I'm a big believer in the Law of Attraction. **It works** in vast and mysterious ways. In fact, the phrase *Law of Attraction* has become such a popular belief and term, that it is now included in some dictionaries!

To quote The Urban Dictionary:

"The Law of Attraction is the belief that positive thoughts are magnets for positive life experiences and negative thoughts are magnets for negative life experiences."

This definition supported my own findings that our thoughts DO manifest within our very lives, Positive OR negative, it doesn't matter. No matter how positive we think we are in our sayings or thoughts, the universe picks up on those 'icky' (AKA "negative") elements. In fact, the universe doesn't even seem to comprehend the words 'no' or 'not.' For example, in the statement, *"I am NOT poor,"* all the universe hears is, *"I AM poor."*

Or, when you say, "I am NOT smoking," the universe turns it into, "I am smoking."

"I no longer eat junk food" morphs into "I long for junk food."

In response to what the universe thinks it hears, it continues to sustain the poorness of your life, the addiction to cigarettes or the craving for junk food. I know, this is very odd, but it's the way it seems to go. This is the essence of the Law.

Try it yourself. Say out loud, "I do not want to eat ice cream." Now, what's the first thing that comes to your mind? A ginormous double scoop of chocolate fudge ripple dripping down the side of a crunchy sugar cone? Maybe you're more the fan of a huge banana split with three different flavors of ice cream, hot fudge, nuts and a bright red maraschino cherry on top? Or does a thick strawberry shake with massive dollop of whipped cream have your name written all over it?

Yeah, me too, though I'm more of cookies and cream fan . . . oh boy.

Many others, including respected experts in this field, have noticed the same phenomenon and have written dozens of books on this very subject. Others have made movies or traveled the world sharing the Law of Attraction's secrets in hopes of empowering others. To those remarkable trail blazing souls, I offer my personal and profound thanks for your dedication and brilliance that opened the doors for millions.

Really.

My heartfelt thanks to every single one of you.

However, I've realized that it takes a whole lot more to alert the universe to my desires than just making a vision board or reciting positive mantras. Some would have you believe that's all you need to do to have your heart's desire come floating in.

If it were only that easy . . .

First, an explanation is in order for those not familiar with vision boards, a superb tool to help you envision and manifest the life you desire AND deserve. Creating a vision board is a lovely way to clarify what you really desire versus what you *think* you desire. In other words, your soul gets a chance to remind you what is important. I highly recommend creating one if you haven't already. It can be liberating and at times scary to you.

Scary?

It can be if there is fear lurking within that you will be a 'failure' if you don't get what you desire simply because you felt as if you're not worthy to have it all. I've had to hold many a client's hand and gently love on them for a few months in order for them to create one. Once made, they become giddy with excitement at the endless possibilities that now seem to be appearing just for them.

For those that have made vision boards; have you noticed how your soul speaks to you when you're creating it, and when it's completed? Think about it, if you forced something onto the board, it feels – well – forced; if this "forced" item makes it onto the board, it doesn't feel right or complete, and seems to stick out like a sore thumb. You feel an internal argument ensuing from within.

Stop right there and ask yourself this: Are you putting it on the board because it's the expected thing to do, like a picture of ginormous diamond ring to represent your hope of finding your mate, when you'd really prefer a funky ring or even a tattoo that better represents the uniqueness of you? Or, are you putting it on the board simply because it represents a BIG growth jump for you? Like that bold picture of the Eiffel Tower that you selected, for instance, because you never felt able to take that trip to Europe - been putting it off for EVER – but now you really think it's time to go?

These are very different scenarios and indicate different intentions from within. Listen to your inner voice and allow your soul to guide you to what is real versus what is not. If you hear something akin to *"who do you think you are?"* ignore it – it's just your ego talking back to you (we'll cover that in a later chapter). But, if you ever hear something like *"whoooa . . . if only,"* then that is your soul speaking volumes. Go ahead and plaster that word or image onto the board! Once it's up there, you'll most likely experience a huge sigh of relief.

Oh, that big sigh of relief? Just your soul letting you know it's been holding its breath for recognition, and thanking you. Yes, it's perfectly ok to say "you're welcome."

When you are present in the creation of your vision board, you will experience moments of stillness, or "oneness," if you will, that seep in and allow your heart and soul to speak clearly and concisely. In this manner, you allow yourself to simply BE; you allow yourself to dream and imagine; you allow yourself to receive the endless possibilities that can be yours for the asking. As your heart expands, creativity continues to pour in as you create your ideal future. Now open to receiving those very things that makes your heart go pitter patter, you allow yourself to play and imagine what your future can hold. It's a beautiful thing.

Remember, it's only when the heart sings with glee that the board manifests itself in a very short amount of time and becomes a true vision for *your* future.

However, deep down we all know that there is more to the formula of:

"Creating = Manifesting"

Right?

Think about it, if all it took to manifest your truest desires was plastering cut out words, phrases and pictures of them to a poster board, then you've done it by now. In fact, everyone would have done it by now. Similarly, if periodically repeating a few nice affirmations as you gazed upon the board increased the chance of manifesting your destiny, you'd be doing it daily, maybe hourly. Or, if all any of us had to do to make something magically appear was to envision it unfolding in front of our eyes (with or without reciting Abracadabra or some other magic words), we'd all be doing that as well. Am I right?

Of course, I am.

Yet, as I'm sure you've figured out, it's not that easy. Honestly, don't you think there would be a run on poster boards, magazines, scissors, and rubber cement at your nearest office supply store if it *were* that easy?

Of course, there would.

Unfortunately, it's after the vision board is complete that feelings of self-doubt and low self-worth, can creep in. You'll begin to hear, things like, "You'll never amount to much" or "You're such a dreamer – better get real, for *this* is your life." And all sorts of other – ahem – joyous things. Not very pleasant, is it?

This inner conflict results in very little manifesting and, as a result, life continues apace. This ultimately leaves you feeling empty and unsatisfied with your life, all the while searching for various diversions to help forget, subdue or push aside the emptiness that is gnawing deep inside. You keep busy *doing* instead of *being.* Days meld busily into another. There's no chance to stop and smell the roses. Laughter? What's that? No time for such foolishness and idleness. You know you are caught up in the *Doing* Phase when you use comments such as, "where did the day go?" or "I've so much to do today, I don't have time to breathe." or "Are you kidding me, I don't have time for *that* let alone for myself."

Is that the kind of life you desire (the correct answer, by the way, is "no siree")?

Not a whole lot of fun in my book.

Yours?

These whispers, chattering, and yelling from your inner voice morph, and can easily melt into the psyche, and often times it's difficult to discern between these diversions and the truth.

Regardless of how these shake out, it doesn't really matter, for you have thought them and somewhere within there is a portion of you that *does* believe all that it's hearing. This makes it all very, very real because, as you have heard by now, thoughts are powerful.

It's true.

And, it's worth repeating:

"Thoughts have power"

Yes, thoughts are incredibly powerful, just as powerful as those mantras and affirmations that you've been reading about, listening to, and perhaps reciting. Maybe even some of you have gone so far as to print them out and paste them around your home or office; on cabinet doors, bathroom mirrors, workstation walls, etc.

And yet . . . so many of you are still left wondering, "What happened? I'm reciting all of these affirmations. I'm doing this 'mantra thing.' S-o-o-o-o-o-o-o-o-o-o . . . 'is this IT?'

Sound familiar?

Thought so.

Listen to me, now. It doesn't have to be this way. Wouldn't you rather be one of those lucky ones that are truly living *that* life?

That life that gets you juiced up before your eyes are even fully open.

That life that has you somewhat sleepless at night because you're so excited about the present, the future and the ideas that are now overflowing.

That life that makes you go . . . ahhhhh . . . yea-a-a-h-h-h-h, this *IS* it.

How many times have you wanted to shout out to the universe:

What's going on?!

Life is supposed to be full of love, joy, money, health and more!

I've been short-changed!

What happened?!?!?!?

Along my life's journey, my trials, errors, AND successes, I was given a way (thank you, Angels) to trick my inner voice, my ego, if you will. I was shown a way to remain more present and unveil the answers to all those questions and better yet live the life. You know, *that* life that we all covet.

Actually, I didn't know what I had until we moved from our home of twenty plus years and relocated to another city 500 miles away for my honey's work. Unbeknownst to me at the time, this move was just the beginning of this new way of being.

Here's how it all came about:

A young man came to live with us. We'll call him Jim for the sake of privacy. It was rather an impromptu decision; Jim was the current boyfriend of one of our daughters and had nothing. Literally not a pot to pee in. He had run from his home state with a backpack, and enough money to get out of dodge with a bit left over in attempt to turn his life around.

Prior to his joining our family, he had found a job and was working and renting a room close by his place of employment that allowed him to walk to work in order to save money and rebuild financially. Folklore has it that he was with this particular company for approximately two months. It was during his first job that the two met. Shortly after their 'chance' meeting, Jim's employer merged with another company and the location of his job changed. Since he didn't have a car, commuting to the new location was impossible.

Jim was now unemployed.

Our daughter asked if Jim could stay with us and we quickly took him in. It didn't take much prodding on our part (we're good do-bees at the core of things). It also served many purposes; we could keep an eye on him/them, help him out AND hopefully help Jim turn his life around. We aren't that naive to let them loose together. Besides, the guy needed a break and we were happy to help him the best we could.

Jim became our Harry Potter of sorts; living in the finished basement. Complete bedroom, private bath, etc. We willingly fed him. Purchased new inexpensive clothing as well as more expensive clothing that didn't come off the clearance rack so he looked presentable for job interviews and the actual job; when they were offered. We also provided money for essentials, in addition to psychological support, encouragement, job leads and as much love as we could muster given the circumstances.

We gave freely and openly and expected little in return.

Since I was home most of the time, I became Jim's in-house counselor. I listened as he rambled on about the inequalities of life; how his life BU (Before Us) was and I was amazed at times that he was still walking the earth. Literally.

Without divulging his secrets let's just say his life prior to us pretty much stunk. Imagine something bad and it probably happened. Whether it was self-inflicted, witnessed or had the 'luck' of something happening to him. He had over 15 years of programming that the world was out to get him, beat him up, and abandon him so he best take advantage of it and whoever crossed his path before it beat him. You know, it's better to be the windshield than the bug. What a way to live, eh?

What I did begin to notice was how powerful his 'talk' was. All those doomsday prophecies he would make about his life would manifest. All those 'I'm not worthy' statements and those 'I'll never amount to anything.' were happening. Jim was changing jobs quicker than some folks change their underwear; of course all to the fault of someone else's stupidity, bigotry, or integrity. We tried to encourage, support and even bought him nicer work clothes. We loved on him as best we could even bought those insipid energy drinks that he loved, though which we abhorred, just to make him comfortable enough to accept better AND that the world was not out to get him. However, his own talk, his own belief system supported by his experience was the most powerful thing in his world. No amount of love and support from his newly adopted family could change what was deeply imbedded within him.

And it was ALL nasty self-talk.

Underneath all this Jim is a beautiful person that had been severely hurt throughout his short life. We could witness and give testament to this when he allowed his humor to come out to play. On those rare occasions he let himself be and openly share without thought of the shock value. To this day, he still thinks we had hidden cameras located within our home that were recording for a newly appointed reality show.

Jim brought with him a fresh perspective to the family dynamics; helped out around the house and his insights to life gave us all something to think about; that is when he felt comfortable enough to share them. We saw him care for our pets in the way troubled and non-troubled folks can - haven't you ever noticed that we can love on animals better than ourselves and others? He was no different.

Part of the beauty of Jim not being our biological or legally adopted son, we could more easily remove ourselves from any of his situations and become more of an observer vs. participant. We could step out of the drama and because of that could offer different feedback; sometimes encouragement, and yes, at times, some tough love.

Due to his deep programming, life never went his way for long. He could be manic depressive – now I really wasn't qualified to diagnose him medically, but even I could see how drastic were his life cycles. One minute he was on top of the world, getting a great job with a future and the next, he was back at the bottom of the barrel looking up and often times wallowing in the dregs of the universe. His cycles became regular, and we could predict most of them.

We knew he was going to lose a job before it happened.

We knew when things were going to go awry between him and our daughter before they did.

And, that's when it hit me -

Jim was using negative questions and statements without realizing it. It was how he had been programmed since a young lad and it was so embedded it had become second nature to him. He was without a doubt out there swimming in his own ocean and at best doing the doggy paddle In all his years on this earth, nobody had ever thrown him a lifeline. Well, I said to myself, that needs to change.

Since I was his unofficial in-house counselor, an adult he could trust, I did succeed in getting him to use some *positive* mantras, but he thought they were ineffective at best. The power of his embedded thoughts over-powered any mantra he would say. Initially he would say any mantra and roll his eyes. Yeeahhh . . . that sure was effective. I tried various tactics. Show him how the Law of Attraction was working; for better and worse. Of course he knew better and life sucked.

His negative questions weren't any better: "Why can't I get ahead?" "Why does life suck?" And, my personal favorite, "Why am I such a loser?"

As he continued to ask these negative questions, events occurred that substantiated each and every one!

For instance, he'd get a job, with the hope that this was the one that would finally set him on his way. Then, "something" would happen to make him lose the job, always because of someone else's doing – whether it be the whim of unreasonable superior, a mistake that was made by another employee and unfairly blamed on Jim, or any number of reasons that were never his fault.

Or, there would be a falling out between him and our daughter, the relationship between them having become tenuous at best. They would vacillate between 'being in love' and 'hating' each other. At other times, their situation would wind up somewhere in the middle, and you'd think they were siblings instead of boyfriend and girlfriend; even to the point that each might start dating someone else, while both living under our roof.

I'm not sure either one of them knew what to

expect when they saw each other on any particular day. It was a surprise to them, and you can imagine what it was for us.

When a rare positive event occurred and Jim would get excited about something, whether it was a job, motorcycle or even those 'in between' girlfriends, he seemed to accept this new way of being. He'd try to step into the accepting of goodness and new **good** possibilities, and to keep that energy up to accept more.

Skeptically, he'd maintain this upbeat attitude only for a few days, just in case it meant that things might turn around. Of course, this was not long enough for permanent results, and I would eventually get *that* look, the one that silently spoke volumes, *"See I told you this was stoooopid and wouldn't work/last."*

From there, Jim would quickly slip back into his personal oblivion known as the Black Hole, where he'd smoke incessantly and sleep well into the afternoon because he'd stay up until all hours just fretting over things. And, before we knew it, he'd returned to ways that were more familiar, like a worn-out sock. While it wasn't comfortable, and certainly not desirable, it was familiar.

By acting as an innocent bystander instead of converting into my usual parental mode, I was able to decipher the situation and more clearly understand what was going on. I summed up my observations in this way:

Negative Thoughts = Undesired Lifestyle

Negative Questions = Undesired Lifestyle

Negative Statements = Undesired Lifestyle

And . . .

Positive Statements Made Without Belief = Undesired Lifestyle

Positive Statements Made Without Sincerity = Undesired Lifestyle

Hhhhmmmmm, I said to myself, **if** this was the case, why not try this formula (this may have not been the equivalent of quantum physics or even the Pythagoras Theorem, but for me – and maybe for you – this discovery may have been just as important of a breakthrough):

Positive Questions = Positive Actions = Positive Shifts = Positive Lifestyle

Hmmmmmmmm, I said again . . . I may be onto to something here, Watson! After all, this is as about as close I've gotten to deductive reasoning since leaving college.

I began playing, and framed positive **questions** in the present tense versus just reciting *positive* **statements**. I tried out this new idea slowly, ever so slowly. I'd go around all day long, shifting mantras and affirmations into questions. It was challenging, it was fun, and it set off a spark inside of me that I hadn't previously experienced. And, the best part? I began seeing results of the great kind. First, for me, but also for others in my circle of family and friends.

Eventually, I was ready to experiment and introduced this concept to Jim. Every time he'd blurt out some negative comment, or ask why this bad thing had happened to him, I'd get him to turn those thoughts into positive questions. Yes, he'd look at me like I had a carrot sprouting from each of my ears, but he did it. What other choice did he have with me, the "Angel Goddess?"

It took some doing over many weeks and a series of ups and downs, but eventually, some initial successes bred further trust. He moved very slowly, though, as he was like a timid rabbit, afraid of his own shadow. But, positive things soon began to happen and, as importantly, bad things mostly stopped happening. He found a new job, one that he liked, that seemed to have a future; in fact, he even went so far as to call it a "career move." He met someone, and began to make plans to move out and live on his own. He finally reconciled his relationship with our daughter, and there was real peace in the house. The dark cloud that had followed Jim around ever since we'd met him seemed to be finally lifting.

In time, Jim moved away and became truly independent. We've lost touch, but at last communication, he'd been in his "career job" for more than six months (a NEW record in our books), receiving a decent salary, with full benefits and an opportunity for advancement. No more jobs paying sub-living wages. Best part? He LOVED it.

I was thrilled by what I'd learned from all this. Of course, I was happy mostly because Jim had found a path out of the "Black Hole." But, I was also excited that I'd tried out my theory on one of the most negative persons I'd ever come in contact with, and it worked!

Which leads me to the real beginning of this book. Now that you know how I came to understand the power of what I created, and proved to myself that it can actually change someone's life, you're ready to learn the how's and why's. Just remember, we owe it all to a guy named Jim.

iii. *now* we're ready for the intro

Ok, with the preliminaries fully out of the way, it's time to get down to business.

I mentioned mantras and affirmations in the previous section. If you're not sure what these are, they are simply positive, present-tense statements.

Some examples:

I am abundant

I am loved

I am healthy

They are typically ALL about you - which is great - it ought to be ALL about you (OK, you can use "should" this one time – it's a rare exception). Otherwise, how can you ever manifest what *you* desire? Seriously, do you want to live another person's dreams and desires? I didn't think so.

In the previous section, I quickly touched on one mechanism that is often used to manifest one's desires, the vision board. A little more explanation is warranted here:

A vision board is a poster that you create, filled with the life you desire and DESERVE.

On this board, you can paste such tangible reminders of this life as:

Words and phrases (hopefully uplifting and positive)

Photos of:

Your Home: locations, kitchen and bath designs, furniture, art

Your Self: clothing, shoes, jewelry, hobbies, friendships, family

Your Well-Being: healthy, active people, fresh and organic foods, relaxing interludes

Your Abundance: wad of cash anyone?, luxury, faraway lands, the car of your dreams

and of course . . .

Love: hearts, couples embracing, sensuous bedrooms, sexy settings

It's your vision, so anything and everything is perfect as long as you desire it.

Vision boards can be set up as a medley of different images and phrases encompassing all that you desire, or they can have specific themes.

As an example, if you are a car enthusiast, you could make one filled with cars you wish to own, or car races that you wish to attend.

A business themed board could have people shaking hands, stacks of money, signed contracts, awards, etc.

A health-themed board would have such things such as organic foods, vibrant-looking people living an active lifestyle.

A love-oriented board displays all things romantic; hearts, flowers, hot tubs, and candlelight suppers.

Budding or established authors could paste up awards – real or imagined – pertaining to their genre, best-selling book lists with theirs at the top, or names of publishing houses.

Singers could display concert halls, coffee houses, recording studios, etc. Get the idea?

Of course, these aren't the only topics allowed on a vision board. If there is something I haven't listed and you desire it (fishing, dancing, woodworking?) put it on there!

You DO deserve all that you desire.

If you haven't made a vision board before, I highly recommend it. It allows your soul to speak to you more directly and I'm consistently surprised at what I really desire as I create a new board every year.

Repeat, get thee to a vision board state of mind and create yours!

Now, I must cast fair warning once again that as useful as I find vision boards to be, they are not the end all, even though once made, most experts suggest that you gaze upon it regularly, envision its setting things in motion, feel those things happening. Yet, despite all this, guess what usually happens?

Nothing.

No, you didn't read that wrong. I said nothing happens. And when nothing happens, it leaves you to wonder:

Where's my stuff?

Yes, my dears, there's much more to the universal law of attraction than simply looking at words, phrases or photos to getting the life you desire. If only it were that easy.

I know that at times it seems like some folks are just plain lucky, but think about it for a moment; are they really? They seem to have everything handed to them on a silver platter while you continue to struggle for mere subsistence. You've probably have encountered at least one person in your world like this. You know, that irritating someone who can fall down in a pile of steaming poop and come up smelling like a fresh cut rose. I know. Frustrating, to say the least, isn't it?

Now, hold on there . .. you, too, can be that lucky. Yup! Even little ol' you. It just takes some shifting of perspective and a little practice.

My philosophy is that people like the poop divers are simply more programmed to receive than others. There are many factors that can play into this. One key factor may simply be their upbringing. Just think of Jim's story, and how he'd been so negatively programmed that his life just continued along its downward spiral until he came to understand what he'd been doing to himself. For those who are the opposite of the Jims of the world, there is a natural wiring that gives them a more optimistic look on life.

Take myself, for instance. After meeting me for the first time, our new dentist subsequently asked my husband if I was always "so happy and upbeat" (his exact words). My guy's answer? "YUP! And there are no drugs involved." And, yes, I must admit it's often a challenge to live with me. He would know.

Anyway, for those who are blessed with high levels of optimism, odds are they can more easily spot opportunities as they are offered instead of viewing then as something devious or of questionable motive. Furthermore, for whatever the reason, their sense of self-worth is higher than the "average bear's," and things seem to fall easily into their laps.

Yes, these folks may have a head start on obtaining the life they desire simply because they're wired differently, but that does not make *you* any less deserving. It just means that it's time for a re-wiring – a tuning up of sorts – for you, too. Don't worry, we're not talking about setting up an appointment for you with Dr. Frankenstein or putting you through a Vulcan Mind Meld with Mr. Spock. No, my method involves quite a simple process, and doesn't take much. It's quite painless really, but will take a bit of concentration, self-awareness and focused intent to retrain your mind process.

Are you ready?

Horns tooting, flags waving, angels singing . . .

It's ASKFIRMATIONS to the rescue!

When you *ask* for what you want in a positive, present-tense manner, you become more open to what you really want and desire.

AND the best part?

You'll **begin** receiving it.

Intrigued? Read on.

iv. mind fodder

Fodder can be defined as:

"inferior or readily available material used to supply a heavy demand"

So what is *mind fodder*?

It's the term I've coined to categorize and label those endless questions we ask, often in frustration, and to which we are sometimes completely oblivious that we are even asking them. Therefore, a Mind Fodder question can be defined as:

"an inferior question used to 'aid' during frustrating times."

Some of the more popular Mind Fodder questions include:

Why can't I ever make ends meet?

Why do I always date such losers?

Why does everything always take twice as long as I thought it would?

Why doesn't anything ever go my way?

Why am I such a loser?

Why can't I ever get a break?

and so on,

and so on,

and so on . . .

Do any of these questions ring a bell? Probably so, if you think about it for half a second. We've all been there, done that . . . me included!

Ultimately, all Mind Fodder questions call into the self-consciousness an element of doubt, exacerbating low self-worth, and thus preventing all the riches, love, health and joy from coming your way. It's the Law of Attraction at work. You are *receiving* exactly that for which you are asking.

Lovely.

Think of it another way.

Have you ever experienced those times when things just keep going around and around and around, and it seems as if there's no way to get off; those times when solutions evade you, the same crap keeps happening, and more – ahem - yummy stuff seems to join in for good measure?

Have you ever noticed the same patterns keep repeating?

Have the casts of characters changed, but it's the same story all over again?

Does life seem to be a vicious cycle with no light at the end of the tunnel?

Have you even attempted hair style changes, wardrobe alterations, or even moved to new locales with the hopes of changing the repetitive patterns or breaking the cycling all to no avail?

Does it seem to follow you like the lingering scent of a bad perfume?

Doing the same thing over and over again and expecting different results is what Einstein called insanity. I have my own term – I call this phenomenon the **Gerbil Wheel**.

The Gerbil Wheel magically appears whenever you can't seem to escape these repetitive patterns. As much as you alter the superficial circumstances, try to run away from them, or avoid them altogether, you instead find yourself right back where you started, scampering around your personal little Gerbil Wheel.

You may hope that eventually everything or everyone else will get eventually get tired and drop off. Unfortunately, you're the one that usually gets tired, exhausted, and even frustrated. As you continue to run around on the Gerbil Wheel, the complete frustration can overwhelm you, and you often throw up your hands (figuratively and literally) and shout out:

Why does this always happen to me?!

Which is often accompanied by the all-too-familiar face rubbing, hair pulling, shoulders tensing, and – shall I continue? When we ask questions like the one above, we receive answers that directly support each of those queries:

money continues to be tight

'losers continue to show up on your doorstep, winning your embrace for a while, before they disappear from your life . . . again

each project takes foreva, fomented by missing pieces, lousy instructions, unrealistic expectations, etc.

things, places, people continue to be out of reach and unobtainable

or so it seems

The responses you receive reflect one of the Laws of the Universe, which states that each question is answered directly . . . exactly . . . literally. The Law does not say it *interprets* your question or understands your question, but rather it answers it exactly as the question was asked.

For example, if you are frustrated about money and find yourself asking, "why can't I ever make ends meet?" the Universe does not say, "Oh honey, I know you really mean, *'why does money flow so easily to me?'* or *'why do I always have more money than I need*?' or "*why can I easily afford all I desire*?' So, I'll answer one of those questions instead and throw money in your direction and show you ways to cut corners without feeling you're being deprived in any way."

Doesn't work that way. Wish it did, but it doesn't.

I must report that if you keep asking these questions, money will remain hard to come by, bills will continue to pile up in your mailbox, and the financial hole in which you find yourself will only get deeper, darker, and scarier.

Or, the losers that seem to waltz into your life on a red carpet will still show up on your doorstep. Their packaging may change, but you'll begin recognize the same old foxes underneath those attempts to change their coloring.

You'll see the same thing with those hard-to-please and unreasonable clients who seem to suck energy from your business, your employees, and you.

Flip it around, and you'll still be distressed with your belligerent boss, snarky co-workers, or fair-weather friends. You know who I mean. These are the ones who "support" you, but with a wink and the rolling of their eyes.

And it will be the same with health and joy in your life; hard to come by and fleeting, when it does.

Why is it this way? Because everything we do, everything we imagine is energy. Yes, really, everything; money, love, health, and joy included.

That's why exuding positive energy is important to attract positivity in your life, which is really just a variation Newton's 3rd Law of Motion, "For every action there is always opposed an equal reaction." Conversely, exuding negativity just attracts negativity to you.

Take for instance those who seem to enjoy being the martyr – not you of course, but others. We all have someone we know like that, the ones who appear to play up being sick or down-on-their luck, doing the 'it's my cross to bear' kinda' thing. They get attention from all of this and actually become enthralled with being a victim of life.

These negative minded folks throw out such epithets as, "some are meant to be rich, I'm just not one of them" or "I can't catch a break" or "I've been down so long, that down looks like up to me." These individuals are certainly not the ones that will live a life filled with joy or health, much less one of luxury. They will live out their days being discontented, jealous, and even envious, of others for what they see as an easy life that "somehow" eluded them. They love having others join in their pity parties and bitch fests.

This, by no means, makes them bad people. It just helps cement the likelihood that they will probably never live life to the fullest. This is rather sad because what they don't realize is that the universe holds much in store for them as well as everyone else, because the universe is vast and abundant in *everything*. Unfortunately for them, this includes fear, whining, complaining and so on.

However, let's not focus on that aspect (we do enough of that on our own already and we don't need encouragement), but instead, let's focus on the yummy things, shall we? The universe is full of love. The universe is full of joy. The universe is full of health. The universe is full of money. There's no shortage of anything, unless you *think* there is and buy into that mindset. If you do, then that mindset seeps in and takes hold, like a grappling hook, and becomes difficult to dislodge.

Still not convinced that there's something to this Law of Attraction thing? Ask yourself this: Are you driving your dream car, living with abundance, or experiencing true romance? Is there any part of you that is telling you, whether it is in whispers, shouts or screams, that there isn't enough, and all those rich and happy folks just have all the luck?

Hmmmmm?

Maybe you fear you'll be greedy to have life as you desire it. Maybe you think you'll be taking something from somebody else, because there is only so much to go around, after all. Meanwhile, you just want your fair share, just enough to get by or with a little leftover to go into savings.

"Heavens to Murgatroyd"

Why would you believe that wealth is any different? Think of this way for a moment – if everyone's version of the perfect house was the same, we'd all be living in a cookie cutter houses, all of them E.X.A.C.T.L.Y. identical; style, size, decor, wall colorings, appliances, bedrooms, home office, TV etc. That would be boring, right?

Please say, "yes."

If we all universally defined "love" as a humongous diamond ring to wear on our finger, it would cease to mean anything special, right? Keep in mind, if we all felt the same, both men and women would be wearing them. Ooooh, wouldn't the diamond industry and jewelers love that?!

Here's a secret – I replaced my diamond and wedding rings with a tattoo on my designated finger. My husband has a complementary tat on his hand. Obviously we haven't completely bought into the whole diamond ring thing. Not that there's anything wrong with them, mind you; this is just the way we've chosen to display our commitment.

If we all universally defined the perfect place to live, we'd likely all be crammed on my little island, and the cities, the plains, and the mountains would be empty. Yikes!

Getting the drift?

What you want, what we all want is not the exact same thing, but a *variation* on the theme.

We all want love.

We all want money.

We all want joy.

We all want health. And though they may not appear on our list in the exact same order or look or feel exactly alike, we all desire these things and more. The best part – and, my dear, this most certainly includes YOU – is that we all deserve them!

Maybe this analogy will help.

You may have heard of Baskin-Robbins, the world's largest chain of ice cream specialty shops. They are famous for their "31 Flavors." Did you know that Americans eat more than 1.6 billion gallons of ice cream every year, enough for more than 5 gallons for every man, woman and child. Whoooaaa, right? But, how *booorrriiinng* would it be if we all craved the same one flavor, like "Cookies & Cream" (that's my personal favorite, so there)? Can you imagine a world with only one flavor of ice cream? Me neither.

It might be a good thing for ice cream makers to have to churn out just one flavor, but how would Baskin-Robbins differentiate itself from the competition (or Ben & Jerry's, for that matter)? And, we all could certainly have ice cream, as long as it was Cookies and Cream. But, then again, how could we stand out from the crowd by favoring something different, like Jamocha Almond Fudge, Mint Chocolate Chip or Pistachio? Or even Chocolate, Vanilla or Strawberry.

Would you want to settle for something everyone else has, that falls short of what truly sets your heart on fire? How quickly would you tire that?

So, why settle for a life that does anything less than

make you jump out of bed each morning ready to embrace it?

Why settle for a love that leaves you to second-guess it the moment your significant other is out of sight?

Why settle for health that leaves you in pain, unable to embrace life?

Now, some of you may already be challenging this concept.

You may be thinking, "So I asked to lose my job?

I asked to be saddled with diabetes or cancer?

I asked to have my heart broken by that last poor slob?

I asked to always feel like I just lost my best friend?"

Or, you may look at things on a broader scale and wonder who asked for all of these senseless mass killings, catastrophic weather events, or airplane crashes and ferries sinking.

Bottom line? I don't know.

I can't answer your questions, for which there are no definitive answers. I can tell you that I believe that we all asked, as our reincarnate beings prior to physically reappearing on this big ball called Earth, to be part of certain experiences. Though we may have no recollection of this now that we are here, our spirits agreed to be part of a bigger plan to awaken others in love and compassion.

As an example of this commitment, think of any catastrophic event – small or large – and the love and support that pours forth in the aftermath to comfort those affected. These can appear as gifts to the Red Cross, flowers and candlelight vigils at the scene of the incident, or a simple prayer offered in public or private. It doesn't matter how the love and compassion is shown, only that it is offered.

Unfortunately, many times that compassion doesn't last. Certainly some are in it for the long haul of helping others to heal, but as the majority goes, most tend to forget and move on rather quickly. We are a nation with a massive attention deficit syndrome and, unfortunately, there always seems to be some new sad event to come along and grab the headlines and our hearts, even if it's for a fleeting moment.

On a more personal level, these catastrophic experiences can include being forced to file for bankruptcy, the diagnosis of a debilitating illness, or the premature departure from this world of a loved one or even one's self. Again, you're probably saying, "So I *asked* for this?"

The reality is, we have no recollection of asking for these experiences when we're right in the middle of them. I know this doesn't make sense, and is a difficult thing to grasp on many levels, but at the core I do believe it to be true. However, that subject is a different topic for another book.

I point this out here only to illustrate that bad things do happen to good people and, yes, I believe that we have the means to change our lot in life, no matter what the cause. And, I believe that we can all use **ASKFIRMATIONS** as one way to help ourselves, and possibly the world, change for the better.

Now back to our regular viewing channel . .

Chris Alexandria

v. ego

Psychoanalysis practitioners define Ego in these terms (more or less):

> *The part of the mind that mediates between the conscious and the unconscious and is responsible for reality testing and a sense of personal identity.*
>
> *Compare with id and superego*

Whoa . . . even good ol' Daniel Webster concurred that our ego mediates between the conscious and unconscious! In other words, it filters and decides what is valid or not, *before* it allows things/thoughts/mantras/affirmations to seep into our conscious being.

On the other hand, Mr. Id doesn't like the word 'not.' This would explain why when we're told we can**not** have something, or are forbidden to do something, all we can think about is that "something" until we get it or do it!

Try it . . . let's reinforce the concept we discussed with the ice cream example a few pages back. For grins, tell yourself that you can't have red meat . . .

Perhaps you promised your spouse/significant other/friend, that you would give up red meat for six months to help lose those blasted few pounds that haunt you (and help your heart health). As a result, you can NOT have red meat – hamburgers, sirloin, short ribs, filet mignon – zip, zero, nada.

Now that you've committed to do this, why does it seem that every television ad is for Outback, Longhorn, and even Wal-Mart, showing thick, juicy, tender Black Angus steaks?

Or that no matter where you go, there's a Burger King, Hardee's, or Wendy's on every corner, with big signs that shout about their juicy, mouthwatering hamburgers, two or three patties high?

And then, there's your local grocery, which somehow decided to feature its meat department in a way you never before noticed? Or, you go to your neighbor's cookout, and what's he grilling?

You got it, bucko. And, I'm not talking about the grilled chicken breast, which just won't work for you, will it?

So, tell me — now whatcha' thinking about every blessed waking moment and maybe even as you drift off to sleep? A big ol' slab of beef. Medium rare. Juicy, tender and oh, so flavorful.

Understand?

Thought so.

Here's why this happens: the Id tends to filter it out the word *'not,'* which is actually rather ironic since the concept of 'not' fuels our fear. Ego is based and runs on fear. Right? So by saying you are <u>not</u> going to do something, or <u>have</u> something . . . you actually invite it deeper into your existence!

Here's another example that's not food related:

"I will not succumb to arguing with (insert appropriate name here)."

I tried did this for a period of 6 weeks. There was a co-worker, while a nice enough guy, that would just rub me the wrong way. He seemed to go out of his way to push my buttons, so to speak. It was so obvious and blatant, that there was an ongoing pool within our department about who would eventually come out on top, if we ever did battle. So, I consciously decided to take the high road and avoid the confrontation, trying to love more from my heart than my head during that time, and to see what would happen.

Yeah, you guessed it. Things got only worse, and he just irked me more and more. The more I tried to stay away from him and the conflict, the more I thought about it, and the more he would mess with my head. I found myself repeating such mantras as, "I will not give in to his taunts," or "I can stay calm and let it roll off my back," but nothing worked.

Avoiding the confrontation was extremely difficult, and I took many long walks during those 6 weeks. If I'd been a boxer, I think I might have won a championship, that's how much my frustration was pent up inside. But, I didn't really win a thing except a better insight into my own self-awareness.

Those 6 weeks were far from blissful, but they were illuminating. Attempting to avoid things – whether it be food or people – just seems to heighten one's focus on them. Pure avoidance –

even supplemented with well-meaning mantras and affirmations – doesn't work. Remember this as you read on and understand how what we say does affect our daily life.

So, again, it's ego controlling us through fear. It's easy to recall or think of someone in your world that lives in fear because it takes the onus off of you. It's easy to point your finger at someone else and see how *they* live in fear. They've become paralyzed in many areas of their life and truly cannot move forward to take the next step. They use phrases such as:

What if I'm wrong?

They won't pay for my move and the move will cost too much

Who am I to think I have something different or inspiring to offer for clients and/or students?

My entire family has always been fat, it's in my DNA so why bother?

I'm resigned to be in this job and can have a life when I retire

Best get that milk, eggs and orange juice - weatherman says snow is coming!

If you're honest, you do it yourself, especially when you feel tired and drained of energy. The next time you begin to feel this way, or hear those mind fodder thoughts really sneaking in and chatting away at you, take a gander at your posture. I'm pretty sure it won't be very good. Odds are it's become slumped; your shoulders are rounded, your head has drooped, and your spine is curved.

What happens during all this slumping and drooping? Your heart gets pushed to the back and your ego takes over, leading the way. To add further insult, your heart trails behind you, much like a caboose on a train, and fear leads you around by the nose.

Why is that? Your heart is the birthplace of your soul, and never lies to you. It resides right where you feel your heart beat. The ego, on the other hand, lives in the head and, as we are establishing here, is chockfull of fear. Hence, fear is leading you around by the nose.

Ewwwwwww, right?

However, you can do a simple posture alignment. Slide your shoulders over your hips and then rest your ears over your shoulders. You are now sitting or standing with great posture.

In this posture, it becomes rather hard to continue relegating the heart to the rear of the train. Instead, the heart begins to lead and pave the path you desire. While this may not initially change much, it does offer subtle nuances and shifts of your actions and reactions to all situations, thus ultimately changing any and all situations. It's like your internal current has a chance to flow smoothly instead of going through various kinks and droops and corners in order to be heard. Your heart speaks more clearly with you, and you can act and react while being more centered and in the present moment versus being spoon fed on fear.

Always remember this:

Your heart is the birthplace of the soul and your soul never, ever, eva lies to you.

Period.

Remember that Webster stated ego *is* responsible

for reality testing. So let's play:

What do you consider real?

What is valid?

What has merit?

Do you believe in lollipops and unicorns?

Probably not, because doing so is "stupid."

Do you believe in money?

"Sure - it has merit; it allows me to buy stuff. I mean, come on, who *doesn't* believe in money these days? You can use it in exchange for pretty much anything. Yeah, so sure I believe in money."

Sound familiar?

In not too dissimilar of a way, the Id plays a role in our own reality, our identity. Think of your own existence, and consider what your reality is; what has merit to you? What is it about yourself or your surroundings do you believe is true or not true? Which of these truisms do you fear and, in doing so, fuels your ego? Even the most remote bit of fear will enable the ego to jump in, saving itself by lowering your self-esteem.

Everything wants to live, including the ego.

Let's use the topic of worthiness as an example. You feel worthy enough to go into any fast food restaurant, place an order, and receive exactly what you want. It's a no brainer, correct? You feel worthy enough to believe that when buying a pair of shoes, you get a left one and a right one, no? And, you feel worthy to expect that when you flip a switch, the light will turn on, surely?

So, why does your worthiness begin to waver when it starts to get more personal?

Ahhh, therein lays the million dollar question! The more personal the desire, the more emphasis, or energy, you put towards it. The ego picks up on that energy and starts blowing raspberries at you. Yes, I mean the type that go *blfffffffffffffff*, like the good ol' Bronx cheer. In many ways, Mr. Ego is just like a schoolyard bully.

Try this question: Do you feel worthy enough to receive a million dollars?

Do you feel worthy enough to have total bliss?

Do you feel worthy enough to have your perfect job, home, car, and mate?

If there was *any* hesitation, any sense of stammering, anything short of you promptly saying YES in answering any of these questions, your ego is blowing those raspberries at you and that Doubting Thomas of self-worth has come into play, preventing you from having any of what you really want.

I do mean *any.* It's okay to admit it. You are human after all, and as a human, you're going to have ego until the day you skip over to the other side. It's merely a fact of life.

Humans have egos. It's all part of what I believe, that we are all perfectly imperfect (unless, of course, you happen to be Mary Poppins).

Now that you've hopefully come to terms that you're not perfect, go back and look at those questions one more time.

Do you feel worthy enough to receive a million dollars?

Do you feel worthy enough to have total bliss?

Do you feel worthy enough to have your perfect job, home, car, and mate?

Do you still have any sense of hesitation, anything less than TOTAL acceptance in receiving exactly everything you desire?

Thought so. And, honestly, I do, too, at various levels.

Let's continue . . .

How does the ego play into living *that* life you desire and deserve? It plays into it more than anyone of us may understand, but we're getting better. One thing that has come to light is that the ego LOVES to argue. It is beautifully equipped to argue with statements, silent or verbal. It's got a set of lungs to prove it. If you make a negative statement – "I'm a loser," for instance – it just sits back and lets you have all the fun, encouraging you to just dig yourself deeper into your black hole. You are now feeding the tiger within. Why would it stop its quest for survival?

That's why it's better to try and use positive statements and affirmations – you know, those phrases like:

"I am powerful."

"I am strong."

"I have a great life."

"I am at peace."

"I am abundant."

These statements are strong, powerful, positive, and they're a *step* in the right direction. Anything to get you out of the "oh woe is me" trap into which negative statements can drag us is a positive step ahead. However, I've found that relying solely on using affirmations and mantras is inadequate, in most cases. They don't always work. It's sad, but true.

Remember, even positive affirmations and mantras are still *statements*, and since the ego loves to argue, what better buffet from which to choose than a positive statement – a mantra or affirmation smorgasbord, you might call it.

Are you beginning to see the light?

Let's use one of those mantras above as an example of how ego steps in to 'play' with us:

You State	**Ego Responds**
I am abundant.	*HA! Looked at your checkbook lately?*
I AM abundant.	*Yeahhhh.... sure you are - that's what all those bills tell you, right?*
I AM ABUNDANT!	*Nah...You're just a poor slob trying to make ends meet. Gotcha!*

And so on.

Here's another example:

During your life, how many lottery tickets have you purchased? Did you ever use an affirmation to declare, 'I've got the winning ticket!'? You're not the only one. And, if everyone who bought a lottery ticket then claimed they now held the winning ticket <u>really believed it</u>, meaning they felt <u>worthy to win</u>, there would be no lottery.

This is because *everyone* would get the winning numbers and the lottery would be bankrupt! At the least, they'd all be like those unfortunate players in that Jim Carrey movie, *Bruce Almighty* when, as God, he grants everyone's wish to win the lottery, leaving mere pennies for each winner.

That's how powerful we are. That's how powerful *you* are.

What usually happens, though, when you recite a mantra in which you don't really believe, I mean *deep-down-in-your-gut* believe, your ego, the *birthplace of fear*, once again blows "raspberries" at you. As if that wasn't enough, it then shouts in your ear, getting deep into your mind with other phrases like:

"WHO do you think you are?"

or

"Yeah, suuuure you deserve that."

or

*"HA! If you're soo great,
why don't you have more friends
(or clients, customers, supporters)?"*

or when it begins to masquerade as the green-eyed

monster and those Mind Fodder Questions emerge, such as:

'why can't I get opportunities like that?'

or

'she/he/they are soooo lucky, why can't I get that kind of break?'

or

'they look like the perfect couple, why doesn't he/she treat me better?'

Any of those sound familiar?

In other words, we should now all know and understand:

Ego = Master
of Raspberry Blowing

These raspberry blowing comments from the "Ego Gallery," or anything akin to them, override anything we positively state, thus rendering any attempt by which we try to make our life better null and void. Not sure if what you're hearing is from the Ego Gallery? Ask yourself these questions, then:

Does it make you squirm?

Does it make you lonely?

Does it make you feel less than?

Does it make you feel defeated?

Does it seem to put you in 'your place'?

If you answered "yes" to any of these, then it's the ego keeping you down. It's that simple.

ANY statement you hear or feeling you get internally that is not filled with positivity, joy and cheer is ego. Any statement or feeling you get that twists your gut into knots is ego. Any statement or feeling you get that quickly has you hanging your head in shame is ego. Ego is a mean little bugger and doesn't cotton to change of any kind, unless, of course, the change is expanding its power over you.

Ego can manifest in the form of other's 'helping' you. How many times have you stated that you are on a diet and folks congratulate you only to offer you some sort of sweet the next time you're together?

Ego.

Or you give up drinking and they invite you out for a quick one?

Ego.

Or you apply to college or a trade school to advance yourself only to hear that you are getting uppity?

All these, and so much more, my friend, is ego pouring forth from another's mouth.

Keep in mind that since you are human, you have ego. We all do. Remember that you will continue to have an ego until the day you drop dead. However, it's up to you how much power you give it, *or not*.

Take into consideration that if there is even a sliver or a morsel of unworthy feelings when you state something, your ego will jump in, blast open the hole and -- you got it – blows those awful raspberries at you *(blffffffffffffff)"* thus nulling and voiding any positive statement, mantra, or affirmation (or whatever you wish to call it) you make, no matter how long you declare it, no matter how loud you declare it, no matter how fancy you declare it.

YAY for ego!

So, can you trick ego into shutting up?

Yes. It's quite simple, really.

Ask a question

The ego is just not equipped to answer questions. It's equipped to argue and blow raspberries at *statements*.

Think about it, do you *argue* when someone asks you a *question*? Nope.

You answer the question, depending how it's asked.

Same goes for ego.

Therefore, when you ask a question about yourself and your universe, the ego metaphorically throws up its hands and admits:

I got nothin'.

Hey Universe?

You're up!

So, my dears, the easy way to get around the ego's snarky means of generating fear and self-doubt is to just ask a question. A question, not a statement?

"Really?" you're probably asking. "Is that all it takes?"

Well, yes, but these questions have to be asked in a specific way, and with specific intent. It's time to let you in on my secret. It's time for . . .

Chris Alexandria

vi. Askfirmations defined

Finally, here it is . . . . wait for it . . . .

Dada dat ta daaaaaaaaaaa!

THE moment you have been waiting for.

Presenting: **ASKFIRMATIONS!**

What **IS** an **ASKFIRMATION** and why is it so different from mantras and affirmations?

So glad you asked.

The answer is quite simple really.

An **ASKFIRMATION** IS:

A positive, present-tense question, typically starting with 'why' or 'how'.

Tossing the word 'easy' in as often as possible is a great idea as well - after all, don't humans tend to make things more difficult than need be? It's the old adage – anything worth having you have to work *hard* for it. Let's counter-attack with "easy" whenever possible.

In essence, think of it as a mantra expressed in the form of a question.

Hence, **ASKFIRMATION** . . .

Get it?

Why is this significant?

As mentioned in the last section, the ego is ill-equipped to answer any question, especially those that are asked in an **ASKFIRMATION**. When so confronted, it figuratively throws up its hands and says, "I got nothin'." Discouraged, it goes and sits in the corner, has a lollipop, and sulks.

Now, don't confuse these positively-crafted questions with those negatively-oriented mind fodder ones, on which the ego just loves to feed itself. It doesn't answer these questions either, but since they're of the fodder variety, it feeds the beast know as ego. The beast also enjoys munching away on plain, direct statements. Here's an example of an interchange between positive statements or mantras and the ego just to drive our point home:

Mantra	**Ego**
I am at peace.	*No, you're not.*
Yes, I AM at peace.	*You are soooooo not at peace.*
YES, I AM AT PEACE (your mind 'voice' even begins to raise an octave).	*He heee, gotcha.* *And you are still sooo not at peace.*

Finally, you give up and shout, "ARRRHGGGG!!!! (accompanied, perhaps, by a few choice expletives thrown in for good measure)."

Now imagine the same kind of scenario using **ASKFIRMATIONS**:

ASKFIRMATION	<u>Ego</u>
Why am I so at peace?	*Chirp, chirp* *(crickets chirping)*
Ahhh . . . why is life so peaceful?	*SILENCE*
You say nothing, but feel your shoulders begin to melt.	*DEAD SILENCE*

Eyes soften.

Heart slows.

Breathing deepens.

You ARE at peace

Isn't life grand?

To repeat the obvious, an **ASKFIRMATION** is a mantra or affirmation expressed in the form of a *question*.

That simple.

You can turn any of your mantras or affirmations into an **ASKFIRMATION**.

Try it.

By asking a question, the "ego-arguing" is non-existent.

Want to know one of the beautiful things about **ASKFIRMATIONS**?

There is no need
to find an answer!

Remember, one of the many Laws of the Universe states that IT supports and answers each and every question you ask, much like those – ahem – glorious mind fodder questions that you simply ask without really looking for answers. The universe answers you, nevertheless. But, when you pose an **ASKFIRMATION**, for which you truly desire an answer, it provides one, as well. In so answering,

It shows you why you are at peace.

It shows you why you are supported.

It shows you why you are so very worthy of everything you truly desire for *your* life.

The pressure loosens its grip on those tense shoulders. Answers are provided with greater clarity and quicker ease than you can possibly imagine.

In fact, just recently, a woman posted on Twitter, requesting I show her how to ask the angels for help. I gave her an **ASKFIRMATION** specific for her situation, and she responded later that day that all had been resolved! Yes, just that fast.

Pretty cool, huh?

Let's repeat this important fact:

There is no need to search for answers. Simply ask, and the magic begins to unfold. By allowing the universe to answer, you get to eliminate another item from your to-do list. Allow yourself to relax and enjoy what is now being presented to you in a variety of ways.

How quickly? That depends.

One could use an **ASKFIRMATION** to help find a perfect parking spot - that typically can happen rather quickly. If you desire to have your career truly 'take off,' this may take a bit more time (repeat MAY), as the universe is answering the many details to get you where you wish to be. It's busy lining up the right job, folks, benefits, etc. that meet your exact desires.

We'll go into more specific **ASKFIRMATIONS** in a later chapter, but to start, I first want to share the power of the system.

One of my personal favorites, and from which we could all benefit:

'Why is it safe for me to be me?"

I started saying this particular **ASKFIRMATION** in late spring, 2012. I've shared with you a bit of my upbringing, so you understand my reluctance to show my true colors for quite a long time. For so many years, I just never felt safe in doing so.

Coming up with this **ASKFIRMATION** was a game changer for me and, upon reflection, a no brainer.

We have dear friends – K & G, we call them – who live about 500 miles away. As such, we only get to visit with them a couple of times a year, at most. They often make the trek to our island to relax by the sea with us around the July 4th holiday. This particular year was no different, and they drove down in July. We had a blast, as usual, filled with sun, sand, good food, and good conversation, capped off by my honey's annual fireworks and Sousa-march extravaganza on Independence Day.

Just a few months later, we traveled up to their neck of the woods to enjoy a little bit of a New England autumn. It was in October, just a mere three months after we'd last seen each other. As we were sitting in their kitchen, jawing over a cup of coffee, K takes a hard look at my feet. Then, her head scans up and looks at me in the face. She does this a few times in quick succession. Finally, I asked her if there was something wrong, like maybe I had dog poo on my shoe.

"Nope, you don't," she said. "In fact, I was just looking at the heels on your shoes."

"So? Okaaay . . . what about them?" I asked (I was wearing shoes with only the slightest of a heel).

"They aren't that tall, are they?" K asked.

"Aaand . . .?" said I, now completely confused on where this was going.

"You've grown taller since we saw you in July!"

"Really?" I was completely dumbfounded.

"Oh yes! You're taller than I've ever known you!" More importantly, she added, "You're walking more in your power than I've ever seen you."

'Hmmm,' I thought to myself, not really knowing what to make of it. So I just put the whole conversation in the *file* and forgot about it until a month later. We had family over for Thanksgiving, our annual gathering of the clan, over which I preside as Chief Kitchen Goddess. I do all the cooking, but not any clean-up (isn't life lovely?)

Well, my brother-in-law shows up that morning (YES, it's an ALL DAY AFFAIR), gives me a hug and asks, "how ya doin' *tall* sis?"

Now this may not seem noteworthy since he has always been a *tad* shorter than me. However, in the 25+ years in which I've been married to his adorable brother, he has never called me "tall!" Never hinted at it, referred to it or anything close to it.

"Tall," he said.

Hmmm . . .

Maybe I was feeling safer to be me than I ever have.

As the saying goes, the third time must be the charm, because the clincher happened when we were at a holistic and metaphysical exposition, and the beautiful vendor across the aisle asked me how I got to be so "tall!"

There was that word again. Hmmmm . . . maybe I *had* gotten taller!

However, the icing was yet to be added to this formula (okay, forgive me the mixed metaphor). I went to the doctor and, as typical; they measured my height and weighed me. Wasn't I surprised to find that I had GROWN one full inch since my last visit! I thought I'd stopped growing by the time I turned 19 or 20 or something; at least I think that's the normal case. Now, I don't know about you, but I find that extremely cool.

Now before you start thinking or trying to rationalize this growth spurt of mine, let's just put it to rest: I studied ballet for eleven years, I do yoga. So I KNOW about and have prided myself on good posture for quite a long time (thanks, Mom). So this growth spurt cannot be associated with me learning how to stand taller. I've been doing it, or so I thought, for decades.

I began saying this **ASKFIRMATION**, but not with the intention or desire to grow taller. I always thought 5'8" was respectable enough, and was quite happy being that tall. No, I began to say *why is it safe for me to be me?* Because I wanted to feel more confident in what I am here to do. I wanted to be able to express my desires verbally with confidence instead of wishing my life away. I wanted to be able to recognize a fellow kindred spirit when they showed up.

Now, in addition to this growth thing, folks are literally telling how much I exude loving energy and how I really walk my talk. They say it's an honor to know me. While I'm not looking for the accolades, but gratefully accept them, I do take this as yet another nod that I am safer to me than I have in a very, very long time!

All of that HAS happened and so much more. We've quadrupled my business' product line in that time, to strong reception and interest from customers and wholesale outlets. My first book, *Have You Ever Wondered About Angels?* won the 2013 Mom's Choice Award for Bedtime Stories. My clients are the very best of the best, we get each other, AND we are seeing results in their universe. I'm being searched out not only for radio shows, live events, and have been a key note speaker on many occasions.

The bottom line is this: I am more confident and sure of what I am to do in this life than ever before, and I can share that with you while looking you straight in the eye. I no longer try to deflect or divert attention away from myself when asked what I do. THAT'S the best part. The growing taller thing? The random folks confirming it thing? Just cool side effects.

And, I fully believe this can happen to you too.

Remember to ask:

Why is it safe for me to be me?

But, also remember that the answer doesn't always come in the form you want or expect. Just allow the universe to show you its answer in magical ways.

vii. the ASKFIRMATION Formula

As mentioned in our last chapter, the formula to create an Askfirmation™ is really quite simple. There are only three requirements to remember:

1) Ask a question.

2) Express it as positive.

3) Use present-tense language.

There are a few – **very few** – caveats:

The **ASKFIRMATION** has to be ALL about you; you cannot make the **ASKFIRMATION** about anyone else.

Do not limit to a timeline or 'window of opportunity'.

Do not limit yourself. Period.

Ok, let's go through this in a little more detail . . .

1. Do not make it about anyone else but you

When using an **ASKFIRMATION,** you cannot create it to alter the behavior of another person. There is such a thing as free will, after all. Therefore, you cannot ask such things as:

"Why is it so easy for (insert the name of your heart's desire here) to love me?"

OR

"Why is it so easy for Oprah, or Ellen or Whoopi (or any other celebrity, for that matter) to recognize my product or talent or work and feature me on her/his show?"

OR

Why is it so easy for my boss to recognize my talents and give me a raise?

It's just not cool to try and bend another's will towards your expectations. In other words, this is not good juju. Often times, if love isn't being reciprocated, then he or she really isn't the one for you. As painful as it may sound, this is true. I had a client thank me over two years AFTER I told her to stop chasing this one guy that she was *convinced* was the one. Obviously, he wasn't worthy of her, and she has since met a remarkable man and is extremely delirious in love *and* he feels the same way about her.

Get the idea now?

Instead of asking the question as in the above examples, you could turn it around and say:

"Why is it so easy for me to attract the true love I desire?"

OR

"Why is it so easy for me to give and receive love?"

Notice the absence of the word 'unconditional'. We've added conditions to love and therefore feel compelled to qualify it by adding 'unconditional.'

Pshaw. Love is love. It's pure, it's sublime. Go for the LOVE!

The above **ASKFIRMATIONS** tell the universe that you are ready. Your soul knows what you truly desire deep down. Not what you *think* you may desire when it comes to love – or anything else for that matter – but the real "curl your toes, light up the skies with fireworks" kind of love. Might as well keep it general to allow the real love to come forward and avoid being fooled by tainted love.

The second **ASKFIRMATION** is used to allow you to *receive* the love. Many are great at *giving* love, but not so good at *receiving* love. In a true loving relationship, you are vulnerable, open, the genuine you. This can be scary, but if you are asking to receive love, you are allowing yourself to feel safe to share the real you.

Having been married for over 28 years (to the same Mr. Wonderful) I can tell you from experience that it only gets better. Even after all this time, we share what we really desire instead of just saying what we think the other wants to hear. We allow ourselves to be vulnerable, give ourselves permission to ask for what we really deserve instead of giving in just to make the other happy at our expense.

I know this sounds like a leap for many of you, but go ahead and try it.

When you put a proper **ASKFIRMATION** out there, you'll soon recognize and act upon the subtle shifts that begin to happen. Perhaps it will be in the places you frequent in your search for love; or maybe it will be in the way you listen to friends, colleagues and – yes – even family, as they talk about the kind of person they see you with.

You may find that it shows itself by someone setting up a blind date on your behalf. Or, it could be as simple as having a cute person sit next to you on the bus, train, subway or as a new member of your carpool.

Maybe . . . perhaps . . . what if?

How does this work?

You make it happen by altering your perspective, changing the energy about you. As a result, you'll experience a climb in your sense of worthiness to receive the kind of love you desire (and deserve), while allowing your heart to be open to its reception. There is no sense of urgency behind it; in other words, you relax into the flow.

We've all seen, been with or maybe been the person on the hunt for their mate. Ever hear of the phrase, 'On the prowl?' Potential mates sense this and run to the hills because the energy is so intense that it frightens them off. After all, there's truth in the saying,

Energy flows where attention goes

If you are conscientious enough to come up with an **ASKFIRMATION** regarding true love, you are sending out the directive to the Universe that *this* is something you truly desire. You are now asking in the more appropriate way to allow your Prince/Princess Charming to enter, be seen and embraced. You are now being receptive to receiving it instead of just dreaming about it. By asking for it come to you, the tension that surrounds 'it' to happen dissipates. By asking, you allow receiving.

Make sense?

Let's move on and look over another very important area of your life. Your career. As for the other will-bending example of having others notice your great work, try this one on for size:

Why is it so easy for me to have my perfect job?

OR

"Why is it so easy for me to get my work/product/service noticed, validated and recognized?"

By using the first **ASKFIRMATION**, you tell the universe you're ready to *have* (versus just *knowing about*) your perfect job. Notice how vague this question is? Wouldn't it be exhausting to list all the requirements of *your* perfect job? Not to mention the aggravation that could ensue if you forgot to list something.

The universe knows what gets you juiced up in all avenues of your life. Let it help you make it perfect *for you.*

The second **ASKFIRMATION** allows a perfect alignmen-t for you and 'them,' enabling your skills and capabilities to get noticed by your boss and his or her superior. It can open doors for that raise, a bonus and, who knows, maybe even a promotion? The sky is the limit!

Or, if you're in business for yourself, this second **ASKFIRMATION** permits your service or product offerings to get into the right hands and out to the public at large. Perhaps you'll find a celebrity to latch onto your product, fueling your business forward, or some angel out there to help you promote or otherwise move your business forward.

Sinking in?

Here's another personal favorite:

"Why am I so supported?"

This is where is gets r-e-a-a-a-l-l-l-l-y interesting. I initially started saying this **ASKFIRMATION** because I was ready to take my business, Angel Chatter, very public and very big. This meant I needed to really get out of the closet and be able to announce to the world –

"Yup, I chat with the angels and help people live the life they desire. Because they deserve it."

Naturally, I wanted my family to rally around and cheer me on. So, to encourage that behavior, I created the above **ASKFIRMATION**. Now, you may think that its wording is rather vague. This is important (so take notes). You'll notice that I didn't ask:

"Why am I so supported by my family?"

Why not, you may ask? Good – I'll tell you: First, this **ASKFIRMATION** violates the "can't include other people in your wishes" clause.

Second, it creates an unwarranted condition by placing a limit on the support I seek to my family alone. This is also a no-no in **ASKFIRMATION**-land. Besides, why would I want to limit the universe's power? So vague it was.

And the results (so far)?

Well, a funny thing is happening on my way to success.

As I use this **ASKFIRMATION** regularly – *Why am I so supported?* – not only has my family truly rallied and cheered me on, but folks whom I had no idea were even alive have stepped into my life and offered to help. And I have gladly accepted their support actions to help promote my business and take it to the next level and beyond. I found the perfect jeweler to make my jewelry. I have found the perfect sales agent to get all of our products on televised shopping networks and into major department stores; more is on the way. I found a great photographer and my beautiful cousin reached out from the other side of the country and offered to model all of our jewelry in advertisements . . . .gratis.

Whether it be through their promoting me in social media, or inviting me to speak on their radio shows, or pointing me towards others with specific talents that can help, these little "angels" have seemingly come out of the woodwork. All in the vein of helping me *because I am safe to be me*, so they *get* me and sincerely and genuinely wish to help.

Then, there are my clients who have extended their support in other, more personal ways. One brought me fresh baked croissants the day after a session;

another gave me one of her favorite crystals, and others have shown their love and support with simple gifts and kind words.

And the magical list continues.

Whoa . . .

It's that powerful.

Oh, don't forget the other two rules – make your **ASKFIRMATION** positive and use present-tense language!   Otherwise, you might wind up asking one of those awful mind fodder questions. We do that enough without even realizing it, so don't fall into the trap and ask one intentionally. That would confuse you and confuse the universe. Can't have that, now can we?

So none of:

Why is it so easy for me not to smoke?

Use instead:

Why am I smoke free?

and:

Why is it so easy for me to diet?

use instead:

Why am I at my perfect weight?

and:

Why do I have no more bills?

use instead:

Why is it so easy for me to be debt free?

Next up:

2.   No timelines

You simply can't ask for things to happen according to your personal schedule or calendar. They must be allowed to follow their own course, and find their own time and place. If you try to set a schedule, that is called micro-managing, a term I consciously run away from as much as possible. You simply cannot force anything to happen. Water boils when it's good and ready. Paint dries when it's good and ready. You receive love, the job, the winning lottery ticket when *you're* good and ready.

Think of my 'supported' **ASKFIRMATION** above. If I had put a time constraint on my request, I would have been guilty of micro-managing the situation. Also, by placing any constraints on my request, I could very well have missed all the juicy relationships and fun of these 'unknown' friends stepping into my life at their own pace and according to their own schedules! My constraints would have hampered the potential outcomes, and more than probably would have ruined them.

In this open-ended manner, as we step more and more into our *juiciness* (*don'tcha* just LOVE that term?), step more into the shoes of who we really are (tall or short heels), we leave ourselves the flexibility to consciously realize what we really want and, just as importantly, don't want. In other words, we evolve and emerge, much like the way time and events unfold, according to their own natural pace and timing.

We learn to trust not only in ourselves, but allow the universe to deliver our order *exactly* as we desire it. At our very core, our soul does not change much, so our orders are always pure. What changes is the package – our body – how we present ourselves to the outside world.

Think of it this way: you evolve naturally throughout your life. As you grow, something as routine as your shoe size changes. If your shoe size has changed, so has the size of your clothes, and most likely, so do the styles and colors you choose to wear. Similarly, your hair continues to grow – and if you're anything like me, so does style and perhaps even the color of your hair; maybe a number of times over the years.

You evolved slowly, on your own timeline. You will change further as you continue to evolve through your lifetime, so why not continue to ask:

Why is it safe for me to be me?

and

Why am I so supported?

Seriously, why not continue to say these two until the day you drop dead? As you change and evolve, so does your comfort zone. Allow yourself to step out of the comfort zone more regularly and comfortably your entire life. Ask for the help and support to make this transition easier.

This allows folks to recognize you the entire time instead of waiting for them to catch up or having the cast of characters switch up. By asking these two little ol' Askfirmations *foreva*, the cast of characters can change along with you as you change.

This also happens with other areas of your life. Similar to your tastes in clothing and hairstyles, think of how your tastes in furniture, art, and, perhaps your expectations of others have changed over the years. As you evolve, so do your boundaries. They expand and constrict depending on the circumstances, and your expectations similarly expand and constrict.

For example, children typically have boundless self-confidence. They have little fear of anything, and are constantly conjuring up magical powers, imaginary friends, and far-away lands as they play, without any fear of ridicule or acceptance by those around them. Unfortunately, these free-minded abilities usually diminish with age, as we make an effort to fit in with the crowd.

And, so, an inner-conflict seems to begin to take hold around the time we transition from grade to middle school, as alliances are built and cliques created. We wrestle with who we are and who we need to be for acceptance. When we figure it out, and find ourselves "in," we initially feel pretty darn good - after all, people are chatting with us, noticing who we are, and making us feel like we belong. Remember those days? We all went through them, BUUUUTTTT we did these things just to go along, to 'be accepted,' and in the process, we left our juiciness far behind.

Think of yourself in this situation – and it may not even be when you were in school. It may be right now, as you find yourself amongst colleagues from work, neighbors at a cookout, or members of your religious congregation. You find that you are somehow different from the others and realize how difficult it will be to adjust to the "norm." In the worst case scenarios, you begin to call yourself *weirdo*, *psycho*, or just plain old *odd* as a way to justify your uniqueness, but these are not very self-affirming, are they (and keep in mind that the ego is back there cheering you on when you make those kinds of statements)? If you continue to describe yourself in these types of terms, you begin to believe in them. What kind of life do you think a person who considers themselves "weird" would be living?

Probably not the one they desire.

Why is it safe for me to be me?

Why am I so supported?

(keep saying these)

If you stop and look around and honestly view the situations in which you've placed yourself, you will understand what you've done and how you got there. You'll see that these people with whom you tried so hard to fit in, to become one with, are not really our true friends. Real friends don't demand that you to conform to their way of thinking just to be with them. They don't offer back-handed compliments. They don't speak ill of those who are not present.

You know deep down inside that this is right, and you've been too long in ignoring these behaviors and how they make you feel because you so wanted to be accepted. Don't you deserve to be accepted simply because you're you?

We've all done something or nothing in order to be accepted. It's easier, right? Wrong. While it may seem easier, the longer you deny your true self the light of day, the more frustrated, discontented and, ultimately, unhealthy you become.

True.

You can become sick, you can become more disgruntled, you can become more unsatisfied with life, no matter the "happy" circumstances with which you surround yourself. When you avoid being very honest with yourself, life doesn't seem right, something feels off, and you get very grumbly and act like an 'old codger'. Get the drift?

Therefore,

Being truer to yourself is easier. It may seem daunting, initially. But it doesn't have to be – ever. You are simply *coming back to you* while stepping out of the box and into your genuine self. All you need to do is ask:

"Why is it safe for me to be me?"

If we eschew these false friends and take the very big step of unleashing our truest selves, we recognize our own self-worth, understand that we've not been honest with ourselves (isn't that sad?), and begin to find the path to the life we desire and deserve. The by-product of this is that the truer we **are to us,** the better the quality of people we **attract to us**. Just as the unfurling of the rose begins, so does the revelation of your truest beauty, essence, and yumminess.

Think of it this way: Does a rose come into full bloom overnight? Nope, unless there's a variety with which I'm not familiar. The rose takes its time. Its opening is a journey to be savored. The rose entices others to notice it simply by being itself and *doing its thang*.

And, lastly:

3. No Limits!

This third rule of **ASKFIRMATIONS** may be the hardest to follow, because any of us who have at some point doubted our self-worth, we tend to qualify or limit that for which we ask, if only to lessen the pain of the letdown when we don't get it. Perhaps you wish to focus on bringing more money in. Let's just say you are currently making twenty dollars a week. You will be THRILLED to make thirty dollars a week or, if you are really a big dreamer, forty dollars a week.

Why are you limiting yourself to even doubling your salary?

What's wrong with triple or quadruple the amount

of money you are currently making? Everyone has a comfort level of what they think they're worth and can safely make without feeling greedy. Why not try the **ASKFIRMATION** way of getting what you really want when it comes to money?

Here's one of my favorites:

Why is it so easy for me to make gobs of money

doing what I love and how I love doing it?

Now, you may have gotten stuck on the word 'gobs.' Good! To my knowledge, there is no monetary significance to 'gobs.' However, it does signify a <u>lot</u>, wouldn't you agree? Not only that, its one of those words that brings a smile to the face.

The universe knows what you are capable of.

The universe knows your material desires – home, car, yacht, jewelry, vacation, etc.

The universe knows the perfect amount of money you need to thrive (simply surviving is no longer an option here, folks).

The universe knows *you* and what will get you juiced up and what is required monetarily to have you living life on your terms.

The same concept applies to romantic partners. Why limit your ideal partner to just tall and dark; a certain age; a specific eye color; a pre-set occupation? I recommend the **ASKFIRMATION** we used before, but here it is again:

Why is it so easy for me to give and receive love?

You may be thinking LOVE when starting to say this, but love can come from any friend or neighbor offering you free food (living on an island, we are blessed to be the recipients of many offers of free clams, crabs and local produce). Others can express love with their offers of watching the children, running an errand or a lending a helping hand in the garden. After all, love comes in all forms.

These acts may come because they have witnessed how hard you work, and wanted to honor who you are. These expressions of love can come just from the heart without sense or concern about their costs; and why would you try to put a price on them in the first place? So I ask again, why set a limit on what you desire?

Here's another example:

Let's say you're an artist, a writer or a craftsman. Why limit yourself to just one blue ribbon or award? Why limit to being only recognized for your greatness once? You DESERVE ALL the accolades the universe can bestow on you.

Why is it so easy for my brilliant work to be recognized and honored?

That's pretty simple, wouldn't you agree? This **ASKFIRMATION** leaves all the doors wide open for *everyone* – and I do mean *everyone* – to recognize, validate and honor your brilliance.

Here's an example: a client decided to clear the energy of her office while her boss was out at a business meeting. Though at the time, she was only a part-time employee, she nevertheless took the initiative to clear the energy because she felt it was needed, and did it without asking her boss' permission. She conferred with me afterwards to make sure everything was appropriately cleared, after which she recited the above **ASKFIRMATION**.

When her boss returned – mind you, he had no

idea of what she had literally done – he noticed how clean and fresh everything felt, and exclaimed that the cleaning staff must have really kicked it up a notch!

She'll inform him one day what really happened . . .

The point is that her work was noticed, and noticed immediately. As a result of this and other successes – fueled by her use of my **ASKFIRMATION** system, she has been asked to stay on full time, with a hefty raise to boot!

Now *that's* a confirmation!

Chris Alexandria

viii. creating

ASKFIRMATIONS

By this time, with the knowledge that you've made it to this point, I'm guessing that you're probably asking, "How do I make up my own **ASKFIRMATION**? Great question, and I'm so glad you asked.

Whenever you feel like something is amiss, or is just simply not going your way,

place your hands over your heart.

As I referenced earlier, your heart is the birthplace of soul and it never lies to you. By doing this, you are symbolically handing your ego a lollipop and telling it to go sit in the corner while you chat with your heart. Since the ego can't handle the truth, it complies. Plus, it just loves lollipops.

As you place your hands are over your heart, ask yourself:

What have I been saying or asking in connection/relation to _____?

Something will quickly come to mind.

Write it down

Do not sugar coat it to make it sound pretty. It is what it is, and this is the no judgment zone. Once you see what you've been thinking or even saying, you'll quickly understand why your universe is slightly wonky at the moment. You *are* getting exactly what you have put out there.

Darn it.

No worries. Looking at that phrase – remember those mind fodder questions – will confirm it. Simply turn that mind fodder question into a positive, present-tense question, and it becomes your **ASKFIRMATION**. Oh, and try to incorporate the word *easy* in for good measure.

It's that simple.

Here are some typical phrases and their **ASKFIRMATION** replacements:

I suck

Why am I so great?

Things take twice as long as they should

Why does life flow with such ease?

Why can't I get ahead?

Why is it so easy for me to live the life I desire?

Why can't I figure this crap out?

Why is it so easy for me to understand?

And so on.

Chris Alexandria

ASKFIRMATIONS at a Glance, by category:

Below are some of the ASKFIRMATIONS that are the most popular, listed by category to aid you. Some may be repetitive within various categories, but are appropriate, nevertheless.

Remember, you now hold the formula in your hands. Make up your own!

self
✓ why is it safe for me to be me?
✓ why am I so supported?
✓ why am I worthy?
✓ why am I so creative in everything I do?
✓ *(keep in mind creative means in finding answers to questions as well as the artistic side)*
✓ why is it so easy for me to take care of me?
✓ why am I worthy of all I desire?
✓ why is it so easy for me to live the life I desire?
✓ why is it so easy to say no?
✓ why is it so easy to keep my boundaries?
✓ why am I enough?
✓ why is it so easy for me to see my worth?
✓ why am I so abundant in love, life and energy?

love
- ✓ why am I worthy of the love I desire?
- ✓ why is it so easy for me to attract the love I desire?
- ✓ why is it so easy to see and embrace love everywhere I go?
- ✓ why is it easy for me to accept love?
- ✓ why is it so easy for me to give and receive love?
- ✓ why is it so easy for me to love myself?
- ✓ why is it so easy to love and accept me?
- ✓ why do I attract such loving people into my life?

money
- ✓ why is it so easy for me to be successful?
- ✓ why is it so easy for me to make gobs money doing what I love and how I love doing it?
- ✓ why is it so easy for me to make gobs money doing what I love?
- ✓ why does money flow so easily to me and stay?
- ✓ why do I have more than enough money every month?
- ✓ why do I have more than enough money?
- ✓ why do I have so much excess money?
- ✓ why is there always enough?

- ✓ what am I going to do with all this money that flows to me so effortlessly?
- ✓ why is it so easy to accept all the good things life is giving me?
- ✓ why does money just flow like a water fall in my life?

health

- ✓ why am I so healthy?
- ✓ why is it so easy for me to eat healthy?
- ✓ why is it so easy for me to be a healthy clothing size?
- ✓ why is it so easy for me to take care of me?
- ✓ (yes this is a duplicate, but wanted to make sure you saw it)
- ✓ why is it easy for me to have a healthy lifestyle?
- ✓ how can I move with such ease?
- ✓ why is it so easy to find my perfect doctor?
- ✓ why is it so easy to find the perfect treatment for _____?

career

- ✓ why is it so easy for me have a successful career doing what I love?
- ✓ why am I so supported?

- ✓ why are my talents so easily honored and recognized?
- ✓ why am I sought after for my skills?
- ✓ why is it so easy for me to know my talents?
- ✓ why is it so easy for me to know my gifts?
- ✓ why is it so easy for me to know my path?
- ✓ why is it so easy for me to have my ideal job?
- ✓ why is it so easy for me to have my ideal career?
- ✓ why is it so easy to complete my work?

general

- ✓ why is life sooo perfect? ....
- ✓ why is it so easy to attract and embrace true friends?
- ✓ why am I safe and protected at all times?
- ✓ why is it easy for me to see beauty in all situations and places?
- ✓ why is it easy for me to be true to me?
- ✓ why is it easy for me to ask and receive help?
- ✓ why can I get everything done with such ease?
- ✓ why is it so easy for me to know the right path for me?
- ✓ why is it so easy for me to see the large picture for all of life's lessons?
- ✓ why is it so easy to feel gratitude?

- ✓ why am I so receptive to receive the abundance of the universe?
- ✓ why do things and people come along into my life at precisely the right moment to serve my highest purpose?
- ✓ why is it so easy for me to be in the flow of life?
- ✓ why is it so easy for me to deflect negativity?
- ✓ why am I so protected?
- ✓ why is it so easy for me to be happy?
- ✓ why is it so easy for me to be loving?
- ✓ why is it so easy for me to be understanding?
- ✓ why is it so easy for me to be abundant?
- ✓ why is it so easy for me to be successful?
- ✓ why is it so easy to be such a wonderful Mum?
- ✓ why is it so easy to be helpful to others?
- ✓ why is my life so easy?

Chris Alexandria

x. follow Up

Since conceiving of ASKFIRMATIONS, trying them on for size and then offering them to clients for their own growth, I am still consistently amazed at the manner in which tension melts away when we realize that we don't have to do it all! I am astounded by the speed with which some ASKFIRMATIONS are answered. I am heartened at the internal strength I witness in my clients, and myself, and the verve we employ to go after *exactly* what we desire because our understanding and our intensions are true to the universe and, most importantly, to ourselves.

There's no shortage of anything. Everything is ripe and there for the asking. It is simply up to you and I to claim our prizes. The only thing holding us back is ourselves and, now that we know how to ask for what we truly desire, there's nothing standing in our way.

Be sure to find us on all social media; Facebook, Twitter, Pinterest and Instagram. We'd love to hear of your experiences and about the ASKFIRMATIONS you invent! The sky is the limit, so there is no limit to how great your life can be.

I wish you nothing short of:

amazing romances and everlasting love

health and fulfillment

your dream home

great friends and family who adore and support you

ASKFIRMATIONS

Chris Alexandria

Chris Alexandria is best known for empowering anyone to explore their greatest potential, and learn to live life on their own terms. Her vision has been to help others cultivate their strengths, meet their challenges, and inspire sustainable solutions to achieve more fulfilled lives. Chris currently lives on a barrier island off Virginia's Eastern Shore with her honey of more 30 years, a dog who masquerades as one of the island's famous wild ponies, and two cats who tolerate everyone else.

You may find more about her and products at her website, www.AngelChatter.com

Made in the USA
Middletown, DE
08 February 2015